First
Facts®

T0057101

Henry Ford

by Lisa M. Bolt Simons

CAPSTONE PRESS
a capstone imprint

First Facts are published by Capstone Press
1710 Roe Crest Drive, North Mankato, Minnesota 56003
www.mycapstone.com

Library of Congress Cataloging-in-Publication Data
Names: Simons, Lisa M. B., 1969– author.
Title: Henry Ford / by Lisa M. Bolt Simons.
Description: North Mankato, Minnesota : Capstone
Press, [2019] | Series: First facts. STEM scientists and
inventors | Series: A 4D book |
Audience: Ages 6–9. | Includes bibliographical
references and index.
Identifiers: LCCN 2018001966 (print) | LCCN 2018005841
(ebook) | ISBN 9781543527797 (eBook PDF) | ISBN
9781543527711 (hardcover) | ISBN 9781543527759 (pbk.)

Subjects: LCSH: Ford, Henry, 1863-1947—Juvenile
literature. | Automobile industry and trade—
United States—Biography—Juvenile literature. |
Industrialists—United States—Biography—Juvenile
literature.Classification: LCC TL140.F6 (ebook) | LCC
TL140.F6 S56 2019 (print) | DDC 338.4/7629222092 [B] —dc23
LC record available at https://lccn.loc.gov/2018001966

Editorial Credits
Erika L. Shores and Jessica Server, editors;
Charmaine Whitman, designer; Eric Gohl, media
researcher; Laura Manthe, production specialist

Image Credits
Bridgeman Images: Peter Newark Pictures/Private
Collection/Mills, Donald (b.1896), 9; Getty Images:
Bettmann, 7, 11, Hulton Archive, 13; Library of Congress:
cover, cover & interior (backgrounds), 5, 19, 21;
Shutterstock: Everett Historical, 15; Wikimedia: Public
Domain, 17

Table of Contents

CHAPTER 1

Henry's Idea

Henry Ford had an idea. He wanted to build more than one car at a time. It would cost less to build cars this way. This would make cars cheaper to buy. He knew more people could then **afford** a car. In 1913 Henry introduced the first moving **assembly line**. Workers on the assembly line built Model T cars. A car frame took almost two hours to build instead of 12 hours.

afford—to have enough money to pay for something

assembly line—an arrangement of workers in a factory; work passes from one person to the next person until the job is done; moving belts bring cars and car parts to assembly line workers at car factories.

FACT By 1927 almost 15 million Model T cars had been sold in the United States, Canada, and Great Britain.

CHAPTER 2

Hands-on Learning

Henry Ford was born on July 30, 1863, near Dearborn, Michigan. He was the son of William and Mary Ford. Henry was their second child. He had five brothers and sisters. William was a farmer. Mary taught her children how to read. She died when Henry was 12.

Mary Ford

Henry started school on January 11, 1871. He was seven years old. The school had one room for all grades. Henry did not like school. He liked studying machines instead. At home he worked with **steam power**. He also found that he liked to fix watches.

A Big Lesson

At around age 10, Henry and his friends made a steam **engine**. Steam engines use a boiler to heat water to turn into steam. The boiler on Henry's engine blew up. It burned down the school fence.

steam power—energy made by heating water to turn it into steam

engine—a machine that makes the power needed to move something

In 1879 Henry left the family farm to work in Detroit. He worked in machine shops and learned about gas engines. Three years later, Henry returned to the farm. He worked part time for the Westinghouse Engine Company. He fixed steam engines there.

"There is an immense amount to be learned simply by tinkering with things. It is not possible to learn from books how everything is made."

Henry Ford

This portrait of Henry was taken in 1888, the year he got married.

CHAPTER 3

An Inventor in Detroit

Henry married Clara Bryant in 1888. They moved to Detroit in 1891. He worked for the Edison **Illuminating** Company. Henry learned about electricity there. In 1892 Henry was in charge of steam engines for Edison's power plant. Henry and Clara's only child, Edsel, was born in November 1893. The same year, Henry built a gasoline engine in his free time.

~1892~

1- John Ash
2- Thos. Blackley
3- Walter Colladay
4- James W. Bishop
5- "Sandy" Sharp
6- Henry Ford
7- John Dixon
8- Patrick Cunningham
9- H. Ward Noble
10- George W. Cato
11- James Sullivan
12- Eugene Lee
13- Wright B. Thompson
14- Frank T. Mather
15- John W. McNamara
16- _____
17- Burt Pettit

illuminating—to be lit up or to be made clear

This photo shows the employees of Edison Illuminating Company in 1892. Henry Ford is in the back row, third from the right.

In 1896 Henry finished building his Quadricycle. This carriage with bicycle wheels was the first vehicle he drove. It was powered by a gasoline engine. Two years later, Henry built a second vehicle. In July 1899, the Detroit mayor said Henry could drive in the city.

Henry Ford's Quadricycle could reach 20 miles (32 kilometers) per hour.

With help from rich friends, Henry formed the Detroit Automobile Company. The first car the company made was a delivery wagon. The Detroit Automobile Company ended up closing after two years. In 1902 the Henry Ford Company began. But Henry soon left the company because he wanted to focus on racecars.

FACT Ford built the "999" racer. It was named after a fast train that set a speed record of 112 miles (180 km) per hour in 1893.

Henry Ford stands next to racing driver Barney Oldfield and the Old 999 in 1902.

CHAPTER 4

Life's Work

Henry started the Ford Motor Company in 1903. The Model T came out in 1908. It sold for $850. The assembly line began in 1913 at a plant in Highland Park, Michigan. Ford's company began building other models such as the Ford V-8.

Henry's company was successful. Workers built 29 million cars by the 1940s. On April 7, 1947, Henry suffered a **stroke** and died.

"Machines are to a mechanic what books are to a writer."

Henry Ford

stroke—a problem in the brain causing a sudden loss of the ability to feel or move

profit—the amount of money left after all the costs of running a business have been subtracted

Paying His Employees

In 1914 Henry started paying his employees $5 a day. At the time most workers were paid just $2.40 a day. He wanted the employees to share in the **profits** of his company. Henry also wanted his employees to become car buyers. Henry's news surprised people around the world.

Over his lifetime, Henry did more than build cars. He helped start schools. He gave jobs to people who were **disabled**. He also worked to help **veterans** of war. Today the Ford Motor Company still follows Henry's original **vision**.

disabled—to be unable to do certain mental or physical tasks; usually because of an illness, injury, or condition present at birth

veteran—a person who has served in the armed forces

vision—a plan for the future

Glossary

afford (ah-ford)—to have enough money to pay for something

assembly line (uh-SEM-blee LYN)—an arrangement of workers in a factory; work passes from one person to the next person until the job is done; moving belts bring cars and car parts to assembly line workers at car factories

disabled (dis-AY-buhld)—to be unable to do certain mental or physical tasks; usually because of an illness, injury, or condition present at birth

engine (EN-juhn)—a machine that makes the power needed to move something

illuminating (i-LOO-muh-nayt-ing)—to be lit up or to be made clear

profit (PROF-it)—the amount of money left after all the costs of running a business have been subtracted

steam power (STEEM POW-ur)—energy made by heating water to turn it into steam

stroke (STROHK)—a problem in the brain causing a sudden loss of the ability to feel or move

veteran (vet-UR-uhn)—a person who has served in the armed forces

Read More

Green, Lila. *Henry Ford's Fantastic Factory: Identify and Explain Patterns in Arithmetic*. Math Master's: Operations and Algebraic Thinking. New York: PowerKids Press, 2014.

James, Emily. *Henry Ford*. Great Scientists and Inventors. North Mankato, Minn.: Capstone Press, 2017.

Internet Sites

Use Facthound to find Internet sites related to this book.

Visit *www.facthound.com*

Just type in 9781543527711 and go!

 **Super-cool stuff!** Check out projects, games and lots more at **www.capstonekids.com**

Critical Thinking Questions

1. Why was it important for Henry to make cars that people could afford?

2. What is an assembly line? How did it help Henry Ford build cars?

3. Why are Henry's quotations included in this book?

Index